# A Visit to the Gravesens' Farm

written by
**ALICE K. FLANAGAN**

photographs by
**CHRISTINE OSINSKI**

**Reading Consultant**
**LINDA CORNWELL**
**Learning Resource Consultant**
**Indiana Department of Education**

**CHILDREN'S PRESS®**    *A Division of Grolier Publishing*
New York • London • Hong Kong • Sydney • Danbury, Connecticut

*Special thanks to the Gravesens
for allowing us to tell their story.*

*Also thanks to the Brewsters,
who rent their farm to the Gravesens.*

*Author's Note:
Gravesen is pronounced GRAV-uh-sen.*

*Not pictured in the family portrait on page 25 are the
Gravesens' daughter Barbara and son-in-law Dan.*

**Library of Congress Cataloging-in-Publication Data**
Flanagan, Alice.
    A visit to the Gravesens' farm / written by Alice K. Flanagan ; pho-
tographs by Christine Osinski ; reading consultant, Linda Cornwell.
        p.  cm. — (Our neighborhood series)
    Summary: Describes the work done throughout the year by a couple
who raises foods to sell at stores and roadside stands.
    ISBN 0-516-20778-4 (lib.bdg.)        0-516-26408-7 (pbk.)
    1. Truck farming—Connecticut—Juvenile literature.  2. Farmers—
Connecticut—Juvenile literature.  3. Farms—Connecticut—Juvenile literature.  4. Gravesen family—Juvenile literature.  [1. Farmers.  2. Truck
farming.  3. Occupations.]  I. Osinski, Christine, ill.  II. Title.  III. Series:
Our neighborhood (New York, N.Y.)
S519.F548  1998
635—dc21                                                    97-39189
                                                              CIP
                                                              AC

Photographs ©: Christine Osinski

Just off Highway 10 and Maple Road is the Gravesens' farm.

Mr. and Mrs. Gravesen have grown fruit, vegetables, and other crops here for many years.

The Gravesens are truck farmers.
They take their crops by truck to sell
at stores and outdoor markets.

Each spring, before planting,
Mr. Gravesen tests the soil.

He decides which crops to plant.

In a special place called a green-house, the Gravesens plant tomato, eggplant, pepper, and melon seeds in tiny pots.

They water the seeds and protect them so they will grow.

In a few weeks, the seeds will become small plants called seedlings.

The Gravesens wait for the weather outside to get warm. Then they will plant the seedlings in the field.

Mr. Gravesen prepares the land for planting. With his tractor, he plows, or tills, the soil.

Tilling breaks up the soil and makes it softer.

Mr. Gravesen takes away the stones that have worked their way up from deep in the soil.

He adds fertilizer to the soil. This special food will help plants grow better.

After plowing the soil with a machine called a harrow, Mr. Gravesen smooths out the soil.

He and his workers put down rows of rubber tubes. The tubes bring water to the plants. They cover the tubes with plastic sheets to keep the soil warm and damp.

When the land is ready, Mr. Gravesen and his workers plant bean, corn, and cucumber seeds by machine.

By hand, they plant the seedlings that they have cared for in the greenhouse.

All spring and all summer, the
Gravesens weed their fields. It is
tiring work. Sometimes, animals,
insects, and the weather damage
the crops.

21

In summer and fall, it's harvest time.
The Gravesens pick their crops. They
sell them at stores and roadside
stands.

The Gravesens own The Covered
Wagon stand on Sugar Hollow Road.
Sometimes, everyone in the family
helps out.

In the fall, after the last crops are picked, Mr. Gravesen cuts down the dry plants. He works them into the soil.

Just like people, the field needs to rest. Mr. Gravesen calls this "putting the land to bed." When spring comes, he can plant again.

Being truck farmers isn't easy.

Mr. and Mrs. Gravesen work long
hours.

But the Gravesens like being farmers.

They like working with nature.
They like caring for plants and
helping them grow.

# Meet the Author
# and the Photographer

Alice Flanagan and Christine Osinski are sisters. They grew up together telling stories and drawing pictures in a brown brick bungalow in a southwest-side neighborhood of Chicago, Illinois. Today they write stories and take photographs professionally.

Ms. Flanagan resides in Chicago with her husband and works as a freelance writer. Ms. Osinski is a photographer and teaches at The Cooper Union for the Advancement of Science and Art in New York City. She lives with her husband and two sons in Ridgefield, Connecticut.